*L*ISTEN FOR THE SILENCE

A Walk Through the Natural World

Clem J. Nagel

Also by
Clem J. Nagel

Prairie Sky Prairie Ground

"When we tug on a
single thing in nature
we find it attached
to everything else."

"Nature is ever at work building
and pulling down, creating
and destroying, keeping everything whirling
and flowing
allowing no rest
but in rhythmical motion, chasing everything
in endless song out of one beautiful form
into another."

— John Muir, naturalist and explorer
(1838-1914)

LISTEN FOR THE SILENCE
A Walk Through the Natural World

©2009 Clem J. Nagel
First Edition September, 2009
ISBN 978-1-61584-862-1

Photography
Alaska's Misty Fjords National
Monument
Elizabeth Catherine Nagel

cnagel@cpinternet.com

I dedicate this book of poetry to
my two daughters, Lizabeth and Susan,
who share my love for the natural world.

CONTENTS

Misty Fjords

blue-granite mountains
tower above vertical faces,
plunge to water's edge;
eagles soar above and
watch our silent passage
where harbor seals and tiny
snow-white gulls share
cool water mist with us,
faint filigrees of hemlock
fringe the edges of looming cliffs
just barely persuaded
to appear by
swirling cloud wisps;
dark, deep water
beckons thin waterfalls
to leave their lofty sources
and become threads to
weave us together
with earth and sky;
wind-music sings
and blesses woods,
water, stone,
and all that
lives within
this aura of
holiness,
whose spirits
thrive and
grace us all.

Water Music

Travelers
ocean-bound
atom clusters
of water
escape evaporation
on gravity-fed
ribbon journeys

Skin Dance
water droplets
dance
across
smooth
water skin, dissolve into
oneness

Cascade
tiny waterfalls splash into
small garden pool
tinkling sounds echo
beneath dark rock ledges
droplets merge into
sunlit crystal liquid

Marsh Frogs

Early spring emerges like
Easter sunrises —

a small fog's breath
hangs in the air.
Fingers of warm sun energy
penetrate the muck, felt

by small waiting things.
Frozen marsh frogs thaw,
their hesitant voices swell as

muted notes of distant birds
thread their way
through the red of
budding soft maples.

An unleashed chorus
floods the universe.

Unending Symphony

From morning into the night, I hear
the symphony. Soft ethereal music
of wind-brushed red pines,
intermingled with bird song.

Distant ravens' throaty resonance.
A wood thrush's pure flute rift
ripples through the evening woods.
Dry string-of-beads song of
chipping sparrows join with clear
tin-horn calls of red-breasted nuthatches.
A robin sings its comforting song,
mourning doves' coos grant peace
to wood peewees, who repeat
plaintive and sorrowful laments.

The woods silence. I sleep.

The wild-jungle announcement of
a pileated woodpecker is my wake-up call.
His cousin, the downy answers
with descending staccato calls and a flicker
laughs back at an ovenbird's incessant
teacher, teacher, teacher.

I walk through the morning woods.

A blue jay's rusty-gate call proclaims
my presence to chickadees who
call out their name to passing
white-throated sparrows.
Flight songs of finches add happy voices,
an oriole's clear whistle rings out.

Late afternoon. I rest from the heat.

A redstart utters its thin wispy song
from somewhere above me.
From a neighboring marsh, hidden
yellowthroats sneak through tall grasses,
calling *witchery, witchery, witchery.*
A least flycatcher makes emphatic
pronouncements to a red-eyed vireo
singing its monotonous preacher song.

From morning into the night. I listen.
The symphony plays on.

As Is

Through my cabin window,
I watch a wing-flash of white,
an iridescent tail.

The magpie lands with a bounce.
Glossy black crown-feathers stick skyward,
three, maybe four — out of place.

I wonder why those feathers catch
my eye, the bird is such as gem as is.
Why does it bother me ?

The cabin window mirrors
my wizened mane, thin strands of
white lie mostly smooth.

A persistent few disheveled hairs
stick up, not ever perfect —
That's it !   The magpie is me.

I pray, who ever looked
at a partial rainbow and said —
      yuck, what an ugly sight !

Questions

does
the sum total
of spider-spun
gossamer —
keep morning plants
from moving in the
breeze ?

no wind
garden stillness,
yellow blossoms
stand tall,
silent sentinels,
a frond sways slightly —
bee-breezes ?

gray crane feather
lifted sunward
held close to my eye —
a rainbow from
ancient light ?

Water Lizard

A small boat plies the bayous of
isolated Costa Rican waterways.
In caiman and piranha-populated waters,
a diminutive malachite kingfisher
peers into the water from its perch,
glimpses its next meal —
and plunges.

Our guide points to a lizard
draped along an overhanging limb,
near to the water.
  It's a Jesus Christ lizard he says.
    Watch !

Spooked, it drops into the water.
Back legs churn.
It gallops upright in a
two-legged comic,
weaving, water-splattering dance —
and heads for
the distant shore.

Scenic Overlook

Drive hard for hours.
Tired eyes glaze over.
Road-crack-glutted mind.
Press on across America.
Eager for home.

Then a welcome sign !
Scenic Overlook Ahead.

Count mileposts.
Slow down, pull over.
First,
a plaque to read.

Then gaze outward.
Distant eyes meet ours.
Endless waves of brown.
Cow-covered, crowded
massive feedlot.

Thankful –
breeze is at our backs.

Never

Would I never tarry
    to see rose blush come to trillium,
listen to incessant, larger-than-life
    calls of ovenbirds ?

Would I never hear
    the thrush's midnight flute song,
see endless white bunchberry and
    fern-littered forest floors ?

Would I never exchange glances
    with deer peering through the leaves,
hear not-to-be-seen tree toads
    trill in the spring ?

Would I never walk paths through
    sun-dappled evergreens and birches,
watch precise flights of hummingbirds
    visiting blossoms of columbine ?

Would I never experience the unfolding
    grand symphony of storms,
breathe in fragrance of dust mixed with
    mind-settling spring rain ?

What if I was confined to places
    where cars multiply and
        swarm over spaghetti roads ?

What if I lived where people plant
       ground covers of tar and concrete
and cut down trees that touch roofs,
       where children frolic on chemical
lawns and never pick dandelions ?

What if I was restricted to places
       where leaf blowers scream and
slight motions trigger car alarms,
       where the sun and moon have
almost nothing to do ?

I would weep.
       And weep.

Meditation in Thin Air

Floating reed-quilts cover
immense bays of
the world's highest lake.
I totter as I pick my way over
floating reed islands
of Lake Titicaca.
Small falcons glide the thin air.
All-brown robins run along the
reed-covered ground.
Wrens sneak through the thick grasses.
Peruvian ibis walk like
distinguished gentlemen,
disdainful of
moorhens' sputtering flight.
Puno teal rise, circle,
land again.

So familiar.
Yet so different.

Great Gray Owl

I

There she sits in plain sight.
Yellow eyes stare
with an appearance of calm surprise.
She misses nothing —
listens.
Bigger-than-life
fluff of feathers,
loosely assembled.
A graceful flying creation.

II

She floats moth-like,
then glides, plunges
into crusted snow.
Curved beak, talons
hidden among soft feathers.
She rises with
a small rodent extracted
from its once secure tunnel.

Betrayed by sound.

April Images

Dawn awakens to
robin carols and a whistle
of a cardinal.
Their songs coax buds of
elderberry and maple to swell —
signals for scale coverings to
fall away.
Springtime promises
of new life.

White gulls
follow farmers' plows and
alight on flat fields.
Grounded but briefly, they retrieve
upturned dormant grubs —
then move toward
northern
breeding grounds.

Early Planting

Dug the over-wintered
parsnips, sweetened
by their long winter sleep.

Space made ready —
for peas, radishes,
lettuce, onions.
Still more to plant
later on.

Cleared leaves from
the asparagus patch,
manure dug in deep.
With spring rains,
green spears soon will
pierce the rich soil.

In the meantime —
the dove coos comfort
as I lean on my hoe.

Sweet Autumn *

A journey fit for the heavens —
months of silent trellis-climbing.
Dark-green vines capped by
billowy, pale green. Bud-covered drifts
wait for just the right time to bloom.

No flowers yesterday.
They first unfold to meet
the night's sky.
Now at morning's wake,
tiny white flowers
grace the autumn clematis vine.
Festoons of upward-tilted florets
gaze skyward.

In the wee morning hours,
I go outside. Silver light on
layers of white petals
cast diffuse shadows and
greet the full moon's brightness.
All open.
All watching.

I know the ocean-waves of
white star-flowers
will linger late into the fall.
Seems not fair
to be at one's prime
as winter nears.

But then it's always
about promise and waiting —
for just the right time
to blossom.

Their presence is a promise.
Always something more to
see and feel in life.

* Written in memory and honor of
Tim who died young.

Musings

Sun-search
coleus
inside for winter
plasters leaves against
window's weak light

Pollination
newly thawed soil
relinquishes
wild ginger
blossoms hug the dirt
beetles rumble
through them

Egrets and Jay
patches of snow
remain at pond's edge
as
a piece of sky
glides by

Full Moon
faint orange sphere
floats in fog
above ice-floe remnants on
shrouded lake
faded dull disk
joins gray mist-water

Rice Creek Serenade

Morning spring woods
ring with calls of tree birds.
Warblers' courting voices
punctuate the dawn.

Cottonwood canopied paths
run along the creek,
its swollen waters
rush
past
me
on
their
way
to
join the
Mississippi.

Raucous, primitive call of
a pileated woodpecker
floats
across
the river.

Goldfinch Trilogy

I

Sun sets low over
   our fall flower garden.

In hammock comfort without my
   glasses, eyes nearly closed.

Garden shapes blend with
   Monet-like blurriness.

Tall sunflowers glow
   with gold; cicadas call.

Yellow flowers
   everywhere.

Then —
   one flies away.

Small fleeting
   bright beauty.

II

Already, lacewings call.
Welcome sounds in late summer's heat.
  An early fall, someone says.

Yesterday I spied her in the maple
by the driveway, small dark eyes
stare back at me, unblinking.

Her bright eyes must have watched
my comings and goings for days,
without my knowing.

Patient goldfinch sits low
in her nest, waiting for eggs to hatch
and August thistle seeds to ripen,

essential seeds for her small chicks.
Age-old synchronicity –
how like us,
      the goldfinch.

III

Patient, she sat on the diminutive nest
through hot breezeless days and nights.
The goldfinch seldom left her watch,
fed by her faithful mate.
Once when she flew,
I saw three minute eggs.

Later, newly hatched babies with
tiny heads and bulging eyes.
Helpless.
Both devoted birds cared for them.

A week passed by.
Real feathers covered wobbly heads.
The second week, two young birds
sat on the nest's rim, another
on a nearby branch —
alert, ready for the world.

Then, no sign of either parent.
Gone after so much tender care.
Why gone so long — and why ?
Later that morning one chick disappeared.
By evening, another fell lifeless
to the ground.

The remaining one teetered
on nest's edge,
eyes closed, swaying slightly.
Hidden in the leaves.
Alone.

The next morning,
I found it
near the roots of
the young maple tree.

Two small bodies buried,
where bloodroot and mayapple
will bloom next spring.

The small maple cried in the silence
with memories of young lives lost.

So do I.

Lake Superior Snowfall

In the stillness —
a raven calls.
Early morning
snowflakes descend
gently.

Arms interlock to
knit networks of
jewel-lace
blankets.

Slight
puffs of air
pilfer
myriads of
connections.

Crystalline hush
of snowflakes melt
seamlessly into
leaden lake.

Stillness merges
with quiet moments
of unity.

Incipience

Outstretched limbs
of spruce and fir
reach out as
heavy snowfall
falls.

Burdened boughs
begin slow-bending.
An avalanche
of small cascades
follows.
Once lead-laden,
branches flex
upward.

Frozen moisture
released to
the earth where
root capillaries
lie in wait
for spring water.

New growth.

da' íísínólts' ą́ą́' *

We stand silent under
    cloudless blue skies,
        where rocks and boulders
    edge the deep chasm of
        Canyon de Chelly.
Fragrance of pinyon pine and
    juniper fill the air.
Spring-green cottonwoods line
    the river that gently flows
        across the canyon floor.
Far above the river, wind sings
    along the canyon rim,
        hushed only by the trees.

The sun moves shadowless across
    Spider Rock, bathes it
        with strong energy.
The old stone monolith
    stands sentinel over canyon walls,
        once home to an ancient people.

Then all is quiet.
    So still.

        Listen.

So quiet,
  we can almost hear
    our hearts' beat.

We sit, eyes closed,
  faces to the sun.
Then, close by
  a sudden sound.
Rushing wing-wind reveals
  their presence.

    Listen.

Just moments before,
  three distant ravens soared
    with throats silent.
Their nearness now betrayed by
  wind-rush through wings.

    Listen.

Sun glistens silver-white on
  wings and backs
    as they glide past.
They skim, wheel, bank
  far below the
    canyon's sheer walls.
Their dives greet
  ledge alcoves where
    ancient ruins cling.

    Listen

Far below, wind-spirits
     whistle through remnants of
        crumbled walls and
  empty rooms.

The restless wind gusts —
    then silence again.
Silence challenged only
    by raven calls and
       crying voices
   from the past.

      da' íisínólts' ą́ą́'

* da' íisínólts' ą́ą́' is the Navajo word for listen.

Places of the Heart

Kenya Vista
Standing on a rim of
the Great Rift Valley.
Somewhere is the
Oldavi Gorge.
Bones of a relative
still rest here.

Machu Picchu
High above the
Urubamba River
cold artesian water
flows through
polished, fitted boulders.
Ancient Inca fountains
journey to the Amazon.

•

Above
the rushing river
little cloud sparrows
pick seeds from
course, crumbled
rock soil.

Perfection in Seville
A world away,
cloudless
blue sky mingles
with azure.
Spanish magpie wings,
glimpsed
from a train window.

•

Fragrance of
tree lilacs and orange
blossoms,
smother passersby.
Aromas from sidewalk
cafes
compete for
attention.
Does it
matter who wins?

Adriatic Night Passage
In fleeting light
over night seas,
a ship-side sparrow's low
rollercoaster flight
mirrors waves.

Resilient Alaska

Silent
mountains, somehow
convince clouds
to nestle
among hanging
glacier-cradles.
Secure.

•

Fall seed parachutes.
Windblown.
Fireweed dust scatters
to unseen places,
take root.

•

Denali magpie.
Spirited,
jaunty confidence.
Black burnished coat,
reflects the sun.
Inquisitive eyes
poised with an attitude.
A get-away-with-whatever-it-can
survivor.

Halloween Land Crabs

High in Costa Rica,
orange and black crabs
emerge from
mountainside burrows.

Time to answer
a primitive call —
the lure of annual migration.

They are everywhere.
Underfoot, inside buildings
where doors are left open.

They rattle along
   in their
       strange
          sideways
             way.

Onward to the ocean !
To mate and
begin life again.

Blank Eyes Drying

Windy afternoon
over shallow pond.

Warm, soupy-green,
filled with life.

Osprey plummets
out of sight.

Beneath water
talented talons grasp.

Then a laborious rise
into the wind.

Bent wings beat belabored
into flight.

Lifts further into wind,
fish facing forward.

Fish does not
foresee future feast.

Blank eyes drying.

Masters of Avoidance

A loud clamor erupts.
Raucous jay-radar commotion.

Two young hawks find a path
through green ash and pine.
Wing their way toward us,
silent in swift, powerful flight.

Jay pursued, they remain
images of grace.
Their short broad wings and
long rudder tails allow deft swerves.
No clumsy clashes of wings
against leaves and intertwined branches.

Masters of avoidance.

Still jay-chased, they drop
to the ground, see us, and crouch
side-by-side in protective postures.
Spooked, the smaller hawk
takes off in abrupt flight –
jays in hot pursuit.

Feigning calm, the remaining hawk
walks slowly across the grass, and
pauses beneath a low spray of dogwood.
She stands silent among low ground cover as
a heron might stand in shallow water.

The distant jay-clamor ceases.
Our hawk flies to a low pine branch.
Sits as if she collects her thoughts
before lifting skyward.

Each hawk,
in its own way —
a master of avoidance.

Moving On

September, almost October —

Late afternoon, low-angled sun
　　reflects off small bits of yellow birds,
　　　　swooping in catenary-arched flights
　　　　　　onto spent garden stalks.
　　　　Moving on.

　Insect-filled birds ready for
　　their southbound journey, disturb
　　　a hawk moth, too big for a meal.
The moth flashes a violet underwing
　then disappears under a leaf,
　　while the birds pass through
　　　　with little urgency.
　　　　Moving on.

Last-to-leave hummingbird sprite
　pauses with each nasturtium blossom,
　　　snatches a hapless insect in mid-air,
　　　　then leaves for somewhere else.
　　　　Moving on.

Soft travel-notes of warblers
　join distant sounds of water trickling
　　　into my woodland pond, soft sounds of
　　　　falling leaves settling into place.
　　　　Moving on.

Fall Mumblers

Muffled mumbles —
just inside the forest's edge.
White-throated sparrows
pass through.
Just once, I hear a
full, clear, whistle.
Their signature spring-sound.

Just once.
Then silence.

Back to mumbles —
the white-throats
save the best
for spring.

Alone

The rust-encrusted farm pump
blotched with patches of
gray-green lichens
appears out of place

among last year's
short tufts of tan grass.
The solitary pump
stands sentinel
next to
the old farm road.

The house
once filled with laughter
escaped the landscape
long ago.

The old pump
remains to
remind passers-by
of what was.

Iowa Rivers

As we approach Honey Creek,
    a wedge of snow geese,
        shimmers in the blue sky
and intersects with
        a white, jet stream ribbon.

A startled blue heron rises,
    sounds its primitive warning croak,
        banks sharply, and departs.
In silence, a small green heron flies
    around a bend.

It is early spring at the creek,
    just two miles upstream from
        where it joins Walnut Creek,
    then the Nishnabotna River.
Twenty-four short miles from
    the slow-moving Missouri
        and its sculpted loess hills.

Waters converge to flow south,
    waves of birds move north.

Water Striders

Agile, they hop and skip
on lily pad playgrounds
then skate and glide

Water striders row
their low-slung profiles
balance on outrigger legs

Sun rests on rich brown backs
multiple feet create dimples
on water's surface

Depressions of footprints
mimic their motion in shadows cast
on leaf-strewn pond bottom

Simple mirrors —
  doubles of beauty and grace

termites en masse

With a soft rustling sound,
multitudes of small bodies
crawl from
underground nurseries.
Gossamer wings
brush each other in
their quiet rush
into the light.

The old house shudders as
they swarm
from every crack,
every crevasse.
They scout for a place
to go
en masse.

En garde !

City of Mystery

Ancient weaving of earth-sky-water-air.
Once jungle-covered, hidden, not lost.

Kept secret by descendants of
Quechua and Inca.

Fresh polished boulders
with tight fitted facets, laid snug against
each other, built on unseen bedrock.
Unfinished puzzles of stone
now lichen-covered.
Aged rocks slowly
crumble into soil.

Wrens probe stone crevices,
drink from still-flowing fountains.
At our feet, rusty-collared sparrows
sort through dried seeds.
Wandering llamas graze on steep,
once-farmed terraces.

Do they know where they are ?

High in the Andes of Peru,
Huayna Picchu protrudes
into fluid clouds,
thick with rain.
Far below the mysterious city,
the rushing Urubamba River
winds toward the distant Amazon.

Our breath
joins the wind's breath.
Cloud mist mingles with our minds.

Do we know where we are ?

High above the river, yet —
far below the stars.

Winter Butterfly

I walk along a February snowy
forest path, littered with
day-bright warming sunshine.
I glimpse an erratic flight.
Did I really see it ?

Again. Unmistakable.
Rich browns, blues, purple
fringed with cream.
It lands with angular wings
oriented to the sun.
Then off again. Fleeting.
Gliding.
Back to hidden bark crevices
to wait out winter.

Later, on an early April
day-of-weeping-box-elder-trees,
I see a flutter of wings.
Butterflies gather to
gorge on sweet thin sap
spilling down tree trunks like
vertical, braided rivers.

Always wondered what
mourning cloaks did —
        before spring flowers.

Liquidity

Understory plants
hug the ground.

They keep forest giants
company,
but stay
their distance.

Nights turn cool.
Leaves descend
to greet the
ground.

The gentle floods
form
sunshine pools
beneath trees.

Earth-return.
Life flows home.

Lake Michigan Morning

Lake wind,
left from the night,
gently touches the shore.
Cottonwood's quiet whispers soothe.
Morning.

Lake wind
barely masking
morning song of sparrow.
Silent nodding of Queen Anne's Lace
greets day.

Early
sunlight meets gulls.
Light pierces down through clouds.
Light touches gull backs in their flight.
Warming.

Shades of
blue abruptly
turn lead-gray. Wind rises.
Fresh leaves blow, song sparrow silent,
Waves wake.

Waves wash
breakwater rocks —
race onto rocky beach.
Hidden bird sings from sumac bush.
Gulls soar.

Quiet —
nodding again,
Queen Anne's Lace greets morning.
Gentle wind, and holy — whisper.
Morning.

local showers

windless
mist-quiet rain

leaves
droplet-adorned

beads of water
hang like ornaments

small bird
alights

unexpected
torrent falls

Holdfast

Morning glories twine and
    reach out to what they can catch
        . . . as does the bittersweet.

Woodbine's tiny coils grasp
    at everything, winding tight
        . . . as does the grapevine.

All hold fast to
    past memories, just like us
        . . . seeking stability.

Bluebirds

They turn in lilting flight,
descend to
trees and fence posts
for gentle conversations.

In loose clusters, never alone
as if they have
a fondness
for each other's company.

Always in my memories,
their graceful flight
and soft calls.
Always they turn blue skies
more blue.

An Oasis Interlude

Prelude
Soon after the basswood bloom,
we go to a natural area near our city.
Totally surrounded by freeways and
housing developments, it remains
a sand plain wilderness of
hardwoods, evergreens, oak savannah,
grassland, and wetland.
We come often, after the snow,
to be touched
by its light and sounds.

We explore silent mazes of
soft roads of sand.
Butterflies dart and grace
milkweed, sweet clover, beebalm,
fleabane, yarrow, mare's tail,
and purple thistle.

Purple vetch clamors sunward.
Vervain's tiny pyramids of blue
pierce the sky.
White bindweed curls its way
around whatever it touches.

Sandhill cranes scavenge among
barely submerged islands.
A heron stands portrait-still, poised to
suddenly spear hapless prey.

Buoyant, lilting,
swallow-like flight of
black terns grace small lakes.
Their deft twists of direction
flash white, silver-gray,
and black.

Song sparrows take leave
with tail-bobbing, tell-tale flight.
A seldom seen cuckoo cruises low.
Yellowthroats' incessant songs repeat
from deep within thickets.
A kingbird pursues an insect.
With an audible snap of beak
he perches again, ready for the next foray.
Two young grouse tentatively
cross the road.

Thistle globes of down
reach for wind in
their search for new ground.
Wild cucumber lies in wait to
enshroud everything.

A shallow, mud-edged pond, crowded
with quiet water lilies,
hosts a sun-rimmed egret —
graceful plumes gleam in a
profusion of white.

Yellow spadderdock, white arrowhead,
blue-flag iris, and swamp milkweed
edge the gentle Sunrise River
as it slows into a bed of rushes to —
emerge somewhere else
without fanfare.

Calls of redwings wash stands of cattails.
Marsh wrens rise within their chattering,
fluttering flight just above the reeds,
drop out of sight, only to erupt
again in song.
A catbird hides its secret song
in the singing
marsh bushes.

An early evening's flock of egrets circle
one lone tree for a night's roost,
give guttural, grumbling calls
among themselves
as they settle down like snow.
The ethereal song of a veery
floats from the nearby forest.
A blue heron's floating flight is
a breath-taking vision,
then descends into
a cluster of cranes.

The low sun frames fields of grasses,
some tasseled, all graceful.
Wind coaxes them to bow and sway,
ready to stand watch through the night.
Reluctant, we leave for home,
carrying this place in our hearts.

May there always be water.
May there always be wild places.

Bosque del Apache Refuge

Sandhill cranes fly
from nearby fields.
Threads of gray stream
through early evening skies,
descend to
sunset-burnished waters.

Cranes join their
reflections in shallow water
among thousands of others.
Welcomed by a cacophony of
raucous greetings.
A ballet of bows,
prancing dances, tosses of
limp weed strands —
courtship in the dimming light
hints of a soon northward journey.

For now, the cranes wait.
Lives secured in patterns
of millennia,
they take their places
in present time —
while they rehearse the future.

Until something within
insists on opened wings —
and moving on.

Hawk Ridge

Kettles of
migrating hawks
swirl,
lofted upward on
winds of warmth.

Fall funneling of
feathers,
on the move
southward.

Trace the
Lake Superior shore.

Lake Titicaca Dawn

Colors —
first appear low in sky.
Deep red,
burnt orange,
soft peach.

Marsh bird calls rise from
beds of reeds —
greet the early morning
bursts of color.
Their hidden songs
mark night's end.

Colors —
intense, but fleeting.
Ephemeral glory
grows pale beneath
tumbles of dark clouds.

Suddenly —
all bird calls cease.

In a brilliant flash of silence —
morning radiance startles
sky and water into
multiple hues of blue !

Birds leave reed-bed safety.
With intersecting lines,
ducks crease the mirror of
quiet water.

Morning ritual
merges liquid and ether.

Day dawns.
A transformation —
        of light
                and life.

Horned Owl Vigil

Under a cold
February moon,
a secluded forest tree
anchors a borrowed flimsy nest.
Silent after courtship,
a pair of night-time shapes
guard their precious future,
under their soft feathers —
two, round, dusty-white eggs.
Ever watchful for intruders
and promises of
meager food.

Feathers Go Before A Fall

Years ago, we crossed an isthmus
onto an island in Lake Wappogasset,
on a beautiful Wisconsin day.
Before us, the quiet, protected bay
was edged with tall pines.

There it was ! A stately bald eagle
perched high on an exposed limb.
White head and tail glistened in the sun.
What a joy to see.

We drew closer.
High in the tree, a light wind blew.
The eagle unsteady, rocked and wobbled.
Tail feathers disheveled, some missing.

Two feathers fell as we watched,
landing lightly on the water.
Someone said its mate died two days earlier,
Found floating lifeless.
*Won't be long before this one
dies as well — it's the DDT.*
So different now. DDT banned.

Change happens. Sometimes with effort.
Sometimes too late.

Sometimes not at all . . .

Catalpa at Rice Creek

Beneath a tree canopy
I look through its expanse
into bits of blue, wispy clouds.

The green network of leaf veins,
not the sky-blue-between-leaves,
draws me to

one unblemished leaf that
startles me with its size —
wider than my outstretched hand.

Veins like finger-pathways,
all converge, connect, convey
life fluids to

sustain new growth of
strange twisted pods hanging
downward in pendant clusters.

A far cry from the catalpa's
spring display of
orchid-like flowers that

greet all who pass, until they
flutter loose, all at once, with
the slightest breeze —

like moth wings released.
It will be like that one fall day
or two, when all its leaves drop.

But, for now —
            it is now.

After a Spring Thaw

Decayed remains of a deer
cling to the creek bank.
Her carcass lies in
shallow, running water;
head at rest on a bed of dry grasses.

Tawny fur tufts blow in the wind.
Patches of dry skin stretch taunt,
drum-like across ribcage bones.

Rivulets' gentle sounds surround
the partly submerged water-soul.

Deep water carves rib patterns
on the sandy stream bottom.
A mirror mocking death.

Fresh rosettes of green emerge among
the creek bank's dried brown grasses
and greet the blue sunlit sky.
Spring warblers cover bare tree-tops
with their songs.

yearning for the sky

imagine something
blooming only within

like hidden tulip bulbs
still bedded for winter

beneath cold beds of leaves —
in forgotten garden corners

pale pink buds
strain to bloom

unable to pierce
the frozen ground

Windswept

Windswept barrier islands
   lie below cold, diffuse-gray skies.
The rush of beige-jade waves,
   crest, pause, and curl
   just before their downward plunge.
Water churns in
   murky turbulence.

Wind-whipped froth
   skitters along wet sand
   as if with a mind of its own.
The iridescent bubbles linger —
   just for a moment.

Sandpipers run, stop, and
   balance on the footprints of
   their water-mirrored selves.

They hurry seaward,
   discover food between each
   fresh new wave's return.

Sandwiched between
   sky and sea.
Pelicans with wings set,
   deftly skim the wind
   along wave troughs.

Sand-laden waves kick
   higher than the horizon.
The earth strives
   to become airborne.

Greeting the air like
   leaping gazelles.

Clarity ?

Tonight I rest.
My backyard hammock —
a familiar web of cotton strands,
cradled between an old white pine
and equally old crabapple tree.
Suspended over a wildflower sanctuary,
my favorite place to gaze at
the distant night sky.

I hear night sounds.
Pulsing calls of diminutive lacewings
punctuate the autumn evening's cool.
Somewhere a crackle among
unforgiving branches,
like paper-thin wings of a wayward kite,
a startled bird's frantic flapping.
Through wispy pine needles,
star-clusters glimmer faint through
murky city-light, starlight that
strains to pierce the urban filter.

Under the night sky, awakening
floods over me like a surge of water.
I imagine myriads of stars surrounding
earth's envelope and wonder.

Does someone far away stare as I do
into their sky and ask
  who else is there ?

A Winter Gathering

Hungry great gray owls
move south from familiar Arctic climes.
Driven by strong survival instincts,
they seek food and temporary homes.

Grays congregate on daytime perches in
open fields near bogs of tamarack, whose
sparse, barren skeletons wait for delicate
coats of spring-green. Dark spruce sentinels
pierce the sky. Fence posts line country
roadsides.

All prime lookouts.

One owl chooses a young birch along the
forest's edge. The tree's slender twigs
tentatively held skyward. Too young for
white bark, its willowy branches an unlikely
choice.

She drops softly upon the uppermost
branch, her huge size masks a lightness.
The birch branch flexes only slightly.
Owl confidence, born of history, knows
support will be there.

Aimless Scribbling

White snakeroot leaves,
dark-green in dim light
with
white lines of
scribbled eating-tunnels.
Leaf-miner playgrounds.

Security spelled out —
safety,
not death.

Small blue butterfly's
scrambled flight,
life lived within
constant risk.
Purposeful, erratic
movements —
pursuers left
perplexed.

Poet scribbles
incessant inscriptions
before
focused patterns order
wayward thoughts, and
metaphors.
Words come alive —

released into lives.

ABOUT THE AUTHOR
A Poet Come Lately

Clem J. Nagel is a published poet and teacher of poetry. He began writing poetry eleven years ago, when his poetry simply "showed up" one day. He nurtures his abiding interests in the natural world, spirituality, human behavior, travel, and social justice — all of which are an inseparable part of his writing.

A lifelong student of the natural world, Clem is formally trained in theology, natural sciences, and spiritual direction. He has a love of teaching others to be attentive to the miracles of nature and to discover their own poetic voice. He offers readings in a variety of settings as a way to share his poetry.

Clem has worked as a community organizer on various efforts to improve services for people and address social justice issues. He has organized boycotts and marched to call attention to discrimination, was instrumental in organizing one of the first counseling centers for teens and their families in Minnesota, and helped form the first suburban chapter in the country for Twin Cities Habitat for Humanity.

Clem shares his long-time interests with his spouse, Elizabeth. They live in Fridley, Minnesota and have two daughters, two son-in-laws, four grandsons, and one granddaughter.